Food Preservation
Everything from Canning & Freezing to Pickling & Other Methods

Table of Contents

About the Book 3

Introduction 4

Chapter 1—Canning 5

    Processes 7

Chapter 2—Freezing 11

    Packaging Needed 12

Chapter 3 –Drying 17

    Methods for Drying 21

    Fruit Drying 23

    Herb Drying 30

    Drying Chives 31

    Drying Dill 32

Chapter 4—Pickling 35

    Basics of Pickling 35

    Equipment Needed 37

    Pickling Olives 38

    Problems with Pickling 39

Chapter 5—Other Things to Preserves 42

    Condiments 42

    Marinades 47

About the Book

This book should serve as a guide to the basics of food preservation. You will find information on canning, freezing, and pickling fruits, vegetables, and meats. You will also discover that other things can be preserved, such as jams, jellies, preserves, and condiments. Food preservation is a way to save yourself some money, and stock your shelves all year long.

Introduction

Food preservation is an excellent way to feed your family natural, wholesome products, many of which you can grow or raise yourself. The first chapter focuses on canning, a simple method for preserving food, although it can be time consuming. It is definitely worth it in the long run, however. The second chapter teaches you about freezing foods, another method for preserving food.

Moving on, you will learn about drying foods, which is also a way you can preserve your foods. In the fourth chapter, you will discover what items can be pickled and just how you do that. Finally, in chapter five, you will learn about other items that can be preserved, and the methods for doing so.

Chapter 1—Canning

Canning has been a method of preserving food that has been around for many years. It is a method that is easy to use and does not require a huge amount of equipment in order to do. While the method of canning might not be as prevalent today as it was in the past, mainly because there are supermarkets available to provide us with the foods that we need, it is still something that many people choose to use to keep their foods nice and fresh. Whether you are a gardener or like the idea of having fresh food available all throughout the year, canning can be something that you can enjoy.

Canning has a fairly basic process to it, although it will seem more complicated the first time that you try to do it. The concept is that you will process the food in the canning jars at really high temperatures. The cans must remain at these temperatures for a good amount of time in order to kill any of the microorganisms and other things that would eventually cause the food to spoil if not done properly. This heating process will also make the air leave the jar and create a type of vacuum while the food is cooling. This is an important part of the canning process because it will prevent the air along with the microorganisms from getting back in to the jar.

There are about two basic types of foods that can be considered canned. The first one is raw pack that means that the food which is put in the jars for canning and processing is uncooked. The other type, hot pack, is the food that you will heat up and cook at least a little bit before placing them in the jars.
Tools Needed

As with any cooking process, you will need special tools in order to perform the canning process. There are several different types of tools that you can choose to use depending on the thing that you are canning and also your own personal preference. This section is full of the different things that you can use in order to get started on your canning process and to do it the right way.

The first tool that you can use is a canner that is a water bath. This is a cooking pot that is fairly large and comes with a lid that fits on very tightly along with a wooden rack that will keep all of the jars from hitting or touching during the process. The rack will also allow the water that is boiling to go all around the jars and even underneath so that the processing will be more even over all the contents. You need to make sure that the rack is available so that the jars do not bump into each other during the process and break.

If you do not have a water bath method available you can always consider getting a pressure canner. This is a pot that is specially made so that the lid will be steam tight on top of the container. The lid does have a vent along with a dial in order to gauge the pressure along with a fuse for safety. If you are worried about the pressure becoming too much and the pot not staying all together, you can purchase a pressure canner that comes with an extra lock for the cover. This type of pot will also come with a rack in order to keep all of the cans from running in to each other and breaking. Each of the types of pressure canners will be different so it is important to read all of the directions for your model before using.

Of course, in addition to having all of the pressure cookers or other methods of holding the jars and the boiling water, you will have to have the actual jars and all of the equipment that come with them. There are a few brands, namely Ball and Mason, that make cans that are specifically made to work for canning. Make sure that you do not use regular commercial jars such as pickle jars, baby food, and mayonnaise jars because these are not ready to deal with the intense heat that you will be putting them through and they will just break. You need to make sure that the jars that you use will be able to withstand the heat along with being able to properly seal during the process.

There are jars that come in all sorts of shapes and sizes so you will be able to choose the one that works out the best for you. The most common ones will be the quart and pint sized ones because you will not have too much stuff in them. If you learn how to use the jars correctly in canning, they will be able to be reused over and over again.

The next thing that you will need to get is some jar lids. Most of the canning jars that you will use will already come with the lid that you need. It will come in two parts and is meant to be able to seal itself. The one part is a metal disc that is flat and will have rubber on the sides to help it seal. The other part is a metal band that goes along with it to keep it in place. You will be able to use the band as many times as you want but the flat part will need to be replaced each time you can.

There are many other utensils that you can use to help make the process easier. The jar lifter is really helpful for after the canning process when you want to be able to take all of the cans out of the boiling water. This is not something that is possible to do with your bare hands so having a tool available will make it easier. A jar funnel is also useful for when you are trying to fill up the jars before the canning process. You might find that it is difficult to get all of the ingredients in to the jars, especially if you have chosen jars with small lids and the funnel will help with that. You might also be interested in having a kitchen timer available so that you can ensure that you are keeping the jars in the boiling water for long enough to seal. Some other things that you might consider getting include some clean clothes, knives, cutting board, and hot pads.

Preparation

Now that you know some of the tools and equipment that you will need in order to be successful in your canning endeavors, it is time to learn how to prepare to start the process. This will consist of getting all of your vegetables and making sure that the jars and their lids are all sterilized and ready to go.

You will want to make sure that the jars that you are using for canning are sterilized right before you add the ingredients, or as close as possible. Do not do it a few weeks before or else the bacteria and other things can easily get back in. There are two easy steps that you can use in order to get the jars as clean as possible. The first one is to use the dishwasher and you will place them into a bath of hot water.

To do this, you will make sure to remove any of the stickers or other labels that might have been put on the jars through other uses. Take some hot water and so good soap and make sure to scrub and wash out each of the jars as best as you are able to do. Make sure to get all the outside, inside, and all around the rims. After you have gotten the jars as clean as you can get them, place them into the dishwasher, making sure that they are the only thing in there to avoid contamination with other food. Place the dishwasher on a sanitizing cycle and let it go. Once the dishwasher cycle is done, you can take out the jars right away and use them or just leave them until it is time to use.

If you do not have the use of a dishwasher, you can also use the boiling method in order to get all of the jars cleaned. You will start this process out similar to the dishwasher one. Take off all the stickers and the labels that were put on the jars from other uses and then wash them with the hot water and soap until they are sparkling clean. You will want to add in the step of rinsing them out with some cool water so that you can get rid of all the soap traces that might be left behind.

Fill up a large pot with some water so that it will submerge all of the jars. Turn the heat on the stove up high and let the water come to boil. You will need to leave the jars in the boiling water for a minimum of 10 minutes before turning off the heat. Keep the jars in this hot water until you are ready to use them.

Processes

Once you have found all of the equipment that you need and have gone through the preparation for the canning process, it is time to get started. The first thing that you will need to decide is what kind of food you are going to can. Maybe you have a garden full of vegetables that you want to can or you are in the mood for some salsa. Whatever you are interested in, make sure that you have picked it or gotten it from the grocery store ahead of time. Also, make sure that everyone in your family enjoys the food. It will not be worth your time to can a ton of one food product if your family does not eve like it. If they do not like it uncanned, they will not like it canned. You will also need to make sure that the fruit or vegetable that you are planning on using for this process is in pretty good shape so that it does not go old during storage.

Make sure to consult your canning guide when starting out on this process and make sure that it is current. Rules for canning have changed over time in the hopes of keeping you and your family safe from harmful bacteria and other microorganisms. You will need to consult with a current guide to make sure that the right method is being used; even if you are using an old family recipe it is better to be safe rather than sorry. Each of the different types of food that you will be using during the canning process will follow slightly different rules which are why it is so important to follow the newest guidelines.

After you have chosen the types of food that you are going to can, it is time to get you prepared. Make sure to wash off your hands as thoroughly as possible and try to keep them completely clean during the whole process. If you sneeze during the process, have to take a break for the bathroom, or touch anything during the whole process, you will need to rewash your hands. You are trying to keep all the bacteria and microorganisms out of the jars and so you need to make sure that everything that is usually on your hands is taken off before beginning. If you are unsure of when to wash your hand, just do it to be safe.

Now you will need to work on the food. You will probably have a recipe that is ready to use. Perhaps it is an old family recipe that has been modified to work with your current situation or one that you found online. Make sure to cut and peel up any of the vegetables or fruits that you are using in your recipes. Some of these can be done a little easier by placing them in some boiling water and letting the skins come apart. You with then place them in a strainer and then some cool water to make it easy to get the skins to slip right off. After all of the skins are off, you will want to remove all of the cores, stems, pits, and anything that you might not want to eat.

The next step will all depend on what the recipe asks you to do. Some might have you cut up or mash the vegetables and fruits while others will need some seasonings added in. Make sure to go through the recipe and follow it step by step to get the best results.

After the recipe is all mixed together, you will want to start filling up the canning jars. You will often find that a canning funnel makes this process a ton easier when you are trying to get all of the food and mixture into the jar. This can be especially true if you have gotten the cans that have the smaller opening at the top. The funnel will make sure that everything gets in to the jar with as little mess as possible.

There are two ways that you can use canning for your vegetables and fruits the first method is to cook them all up and then place them into the jar or just cut them up and place into the jar. It is important to know which one you will be using in your cooking process so that you know exactly how long you will have to cook each one.

When you are filling up the jars, you will want to make sure to leave a little bit of room near the top of the jar. This will be known as the head space. It might vary how much room you should leave at the top of your jar and really depends on the type of food that you are putting into the jar and how much it is going to expand. The recipe that you are using should be able to tell you the exact space that you will need to leave for the head space for the recipe to work.

If you are canning things individually without anything added to them, an example of this is string beans; you will need to take them time to arrange them nicely in side of the jar.

Many recipes will want you to add in a preservative to keep the food nice and fresh for a long time. There are many different types of preservatives that you can use including lemon juice, salt, and sugar. Your recipe should be able to tell you which one will work the best for your needs. Make sure to add in the preservative to the jar before you add in the rest of the ingredients. When you pour the liquid on top of the preservative, they will all mix together by themselves.

After all of the preservatives are added in and you have prepared the rest of the recipe, you can add in the liquid. Make sure to get rid of any of the air bubbles in the mixture. To do this you can take a plastic knife and running it along and down the sides of your jar and pressing the food in. This will make sure that everything gets cooked up properly.

Make sure that after you put the ingredients into the jar, you go through and wipe off the rims. You can use a damp cloth to do this. It is really important that the rims are all clean, especially around where the seal will be because this could prevent the jar from sealing properly.

Now it is time to get the seals ready. You will take an inch or so of water and boil it in a saucepan. Once the water reaches to a boil, you can take it off the heat and place the seas inside. Make sure that you have pushed them down so they are on the bottom, but do not let them stack on top of each other. You will want them to heat through evenly. Let the seals set in the water for a couple of minutes before taking them out.

After the seals have been softened, you can place them on top of each jar. You might find that a lid wand is very helpful for getting the lids out from the water without hurting yourself. If you do not have one of these wands, it is fine to use some tongs to get them out. Just make sure that you are not using your hands to get the lids out.

Once the seals are placed on the jar, you can take one of the metal rings and tighten it on top of the seal. You will want it to be nice and snug on the jar but you do not want to over tighten it. The processing that you will do will ensure that everything stays fresh and good so you do not need to worry about how tight you are making the rings as long as they are snug.

The amount of time that you spend processing the canning jars will depend on the type of food that you are preserving. Some might only take a few minutes while others might take a little longer. Make sure to read through the directions on your recipe to see how long you must do the processing to ensure proper preservation. You can also use the seals as a method to look. If they have all popped down, that means the jar is properly done.

Make sure that when the time is up you take all of the jars out of the boiling water. It is mostly recommended that you use some tongs or special tools to remove the jars since the water will be really hot. If you are doing more than one rotation of the canning, you can place those jars in the boiling water at this time and let them cook for the recommended time as well. If you are done with the first batch, you can turn off the heat and let the water cool down before dumping it out in the sink.

Let the jars set outside of the water for a few minutes before continuing. You might hear a little bit of popping as the liquid all settles and the seals begin to get into place. Let them finish this process without touching them to ensure that the cans properly seal for proper preservation. The jars will be very hot for a while so it is fine to just set them on a towel and let them cool down in order to finish up the process.

Once all of the jars have finished up the sealing process and have cooled down a little bit, you will need to take the time to label them. Get some tape and a marker or some other method of labeling ready. Make sure to put the date that it was canned, what is in it and anything else that might be important for you to remember. This will help you out when you are consume the products. You will know right away just by looking at them which one comes first and should therefore be eaten first. On top of that, if you find a can that has been left in the pantry for a long time, you might want to consider throwing it out just to be safe. After everything is labeled, you can take all of the cans and place them in your pantry.

Chapter 2—Freezing

Another method of food preserving that you can use is known as freezing. This is a very popular method of preserving your food although it has not been around as long as some of the other methods that are available simply because freezing technology have not been around as long.

Freezing is a method that allows you to preserve food simply by lowering the temperatures that the food is stored at in order to stop all growth of microorganisms. This method became patented in about 1842 in Great Britain but did not gain wide popularity until later in the 1880's. It soon became popular because it made it possible to transport meat and other food sources across the country without any harm coming to them.

For example, most types of meats will benefit greatly from being frozen right after they have been slaughtered. This helps to prevent the aging process that seems to occur almost right after the animal is killed. The only exception to this is venison and beef; both of these do better if they are dried out. The meats that are frozen will need to be kept at a temperature that is lower than 0 degrees Fahrenheit in order to get all of the benefits of the freezing process.

Fruits are another type of food that often does well with freezing. Often these foods will be frozen together with some dry sugar or in their own syrup. This helps to keep the air out of the package and prevents the desiccation and oxidation of the fruit while it is freezing.
How Different Foods React to Being Frozen

There are many different types of foods that can be frozen and this is a great method to use in order to keep your food nice and fresh with minimal effort until you need it. Even with all of the great benefits that you can get from freezing along with the many different types of foods that can utilize this method, there are some types of foods that should not be used

To start with, vanilla, some herbs, green pepper, garlic, cloves, and regular pepper do not do well with the freezing process. After they have been frozen and thawed out they will tend to have a bitter and strong taste that is not like their original tastes. It might be better to use a drying method in order to keep these things fresh. Paprika and onion might not develop a bitter taste when they are being frozen, but you will notice a slight change in the way that they taste after they have been frozen for a while. This means that you should stay away from them if you are looking to keep their natural taste.

If you are looking to make the taste of your celery stronger, freezing it might be the way to go. It seems like the freezing process will make this seasoning become much stronger. On the other hand, curry will get a really off flavor after being frozen and it will taste almost musty. It is best to keep all of the seasonings out of the freezer because their taste will often change for the worse and you might not really enjoy the final result.

Packaging Needed

Once you are ready to start freezing up your food in order to keep it fresh, there are a few things that you will need to remember along the way. Just like anything in the world of cooking, there is a step by step process that you will need to follow in order to get the best results.

The first thing that you will need to do is make sure that all of the syrups and the foods that you will be packaging are cooled down ahead of time. This will help to make the freezing process go faster, which is important when preserving foods. Along with that, having the products cooled down ahead of time will help you to retain the texture, flavor, and natural color of the food that you are freezing.

The next thing that you will need to keep in mind is that you should not overstuff the packages. Make sure to only put in enough for each package that will work for one meal. You will have to take the whole package out in order to cook it and it will not be as effective if you are taking it in and out a bunch of times. If you package it all up in the size of one meal, you will not have to worry about how well it is staying frozen later. You can just eat it all and leave the rest of the packages for later.

Each type of food will have slightly different rules and methods for how to freeze it properly. You will need to find a recipe to ensure that you are doing it all correctly.

When packaging up the food, you will want to make sure to pack it all tightly as you are able to do. You do not want any air to be left inside the package and cause any oxidation or other processes to occur to the food you are trying to preserve.

As with canning, you will need to make sure and leave some headspace between the food that you are freezing and the package that it is in. This will allow the food room to expand out while it is freezing. Most foods will need this room to expand, although there are a few exceptions. Some of these include broccoli, breads, asparagus, and tiny meat pieces.

Make sure that if you are using a container for the freezing process, you make sure that they are sealed correctly. You will want to find a tight lid and make sure that the edge that is used for sealing will be kept far away from the moisture and any food. Failure to do this could mess with the sealing and cause it to let air and other things in during the freezing process. If the cover that you are trying to use for the freezing process is too losing, you can find some freezer tape to help seal it up.

Lastly, you will want to make sure to label everything that you put into the container. Some of the things that you should include on the label are the name of each product, any ingredients that you might have added, how many servings are in the container, and the date that you packaged it all up. You can find many of these supplies at the store to help make labeling a breeze.

Defrosting For Use

Once you have gotten the foods frozen correctly for preservation, it is time to learn how to properly thaw them when you are ready to eat them. You have to go through this process carefully or else you have wasted all of the time you spent on freezing them and they might even taste horrible. There are many different methods that you can use to thaw out your frozen foods and this section will discuss them in a little more detail.

Even during the defrosting stage, you will need to make sure that the food that is thawing out stays at the proper temperatures. The foods that stay frozen will be fine for a long time as long as you have done the process correctly. The problems will occur when the food is warming up. If there was any bacteria that was left on the food when you froze it, they will start to multiply when the food reaches 40 degrees or higher. You will never want to let the food thaw with warm water or out in room temperature. It will take too long to get all of the food thawed out and the little bit of food that does get all the way thawed will be in what is known as the danger zone and could easily make you sick.

You will need to decide if you want to have the food thawed quickly or if you have some time. If it needs to be done right away, you can place it in your microwave and then serve it right away. Other ways include placing it in some cool water that is lower than 70 degrees or placing it into the refrigerator to warm up as long as the temps in the refrigerator is less than 40 degrees.

The first method that you can choose is to thaw the food out using the refrigerator. This method will take you the longest out of all the methods and so you will need to plan it all out in advance. For example, if you are trying to thaw out a large item, such as a turkey, you might need several days or more using this method. Even if you are defrosting something that is much smaller, such as some meat for supper, you might need to pull it out the night before to ensure that it is thawed through the whole why.

There are a few variables that you will need to take into account when you are using the refrigerator to thaw out your food. One of these is that each part of the refrigerator will be a different temperature. If you place the food in one spot, you might find that it will take longer to defrost than another part. This might take some trial and error to figure out. Also, the temperature at which you set your refrigerator will make a difference in how quickly the food will thaw. Food placed in a refrigerator that is 40 degrees will thaw out faster than one that is set closer to 35 degrees. Remember to never let your refrigerator get above 40 degrees otherwise the food will get in to the danger zone and bacteria will begin to grow.

Another method that you can use for thawing is to use cold water. This method will use less time than the refrigerator method but you will have to pay more attention that the other method. You should only use this method if you are able to keep the water cool enough less than 70 degrees and it will take 2 hours or less to thaw out the food. In addition to this, you will need to make sure that the packaging around the food is leak proof so that the bacteria will not get in from the air to the food.

You can do this method one of two ways. The first one is to have a constant stream of cool water going over the food from the faucet. This takes a lot of attention so if you have other things that you need to worry about at the same time, you can choose to use the second method. In this one, you will place the food in a container that holds the cooled water and let it sit there submerged.

You will need to make sure to change out the water at least every 30 minutes during the thawing process to ensure that it stay cool enough to do the work properly.

The fastest method that is available is to use your microwave oven. This is not always the safest method though because it will often produce very uneven patterns with heating. There will be some parts of the food which will start cooking before you have even gotten all of it thawed. This means that the food will be in the danger zone and could cause some health problems. You should really only use the microwave in the situation where you will thaw it and then place it in the oven or other method of cooking right away.

Fruit is one of the things that you will need to watch out for when thawing. Often the thawing process can be really difficult for fruit and you might find that the fruit that you are eating has become all mushy once it has been thawed. One way to get around this problem is to serve the fruit when it still has a few of the ice crystals on it.

Fruit can use any of the methods mentioned before in order to be thawed out properly. You will need to remember that you will need to turn around the package a few times to allow it to thaw out a little bit better. If you are going to use the refrigerator to thaw them for about 8 hours to get them to the proper temperature for about 1 pound of the fruit with its syrup. If you are planning on using the cool water to thaw it, you will need to do so for about 1 hour.

You will notice once you get used to the thawing out process that if you have put in sugar with the fruit, it will thaw out a little faster than if you have used syrup in it. Both the syrup and the sugar will thaw out faster than if you leave the fruit unsweetened. This is something to keep in mind when you are thawing out the fruit that you need so that you can get the proper amount of time for the thawing process.

Make sure that when you are thawing out the fruit you only take out what is needed from the freezer. Otherwise you will just end up with a bunch of mushy fruit that you cannot do anything with. If you accidentally take out too much fruit and have some leftovers, it will keep much better if you take it and cook it up.

When you decide to use some of this frozen fruit with your cooking, you will have to remember that some sugar was used in keeping the berries frozen along with the extra juice that will come with the fruit. You must keep these two things in mind when working on recipes so that you can alter the ingredients to work.

Fruits are one of the best things that you can freeze because there are just so many things that you can do with them. One thing that you can do is use the frozen fruit the same way that you would with fresh fruits. This opens up a wide range of things that you can do with the fruits such as using them in salads, ices, sherbets, cakes, and even pies. There are even some berries that do better in making jellies after they have been frozen, such as with boysenberries.

You do not always have to eat the fruit in another dessert. Sometimes it is nice to eat it just plain and out of the package. You can choose to do this even with the frozen fruit and either thaw it out a little bit or completely. They are also really nice as a topping to your ice cream on a warm summer day.

Frozen fruit can also be nice to use as a type of beverage. You will need to make sure that it stays nice and cool after the thawing process, so it might be a good idea to thaw it out in the refrigerator. If you need to, you can dilute the mixture with some water to make it not quite so strong or sweet.

Vegetables are another thing that you are able to freeze. The thawing out process with these will be slightly different than the methods brought up with fruits. Most of the time you will just want to take the vegetables out of the freezer and then cook them right away without having any thawing process. There are a few exceptions with this rule of course. One of these includes corn that is still on the cob. This corn should be thawed out a little bit before starting to cook it in order to make sure the whole thing gets cooked through. Leafy greens are another example of things that you should thaw out a little bit before cooking. Make sure to cook them right after they begin to thaw or they will become soggy and yucky.

In order to cook the vegetables so that they can be eaten after the freezing process, you will want to take a saucepan full of water and place it on the oven to boil. You will have to determine the amount of water that you will use in order to cover up all of the vegetables that you will be cooking. Try to use the bare minimum of water that you are able to since some of the nutrients found in the vegetables can be dissolved in the water.

After the water has begun to boil, you can then place the vegetables in it and then cover up the pain. Make sure to keep the water boiling and separate all of the pieces out so that they do not stick together. Let them all cook until properly done and the vegetables are just starting to become tender. Once they are done you can use them in a casserole or season them to eat right away.

Animal products, such as poultry, fish, and meat, are another thing that you are able to freeze up and save for later. These are kind of in between the fruits and the vegetables in the method that you use to thaw and cook them. Most of them can either be taken right out of the freezer or cooked or you can thaw them up first and then cook. It is usually best if you place the meat into the refrigerator and let them thaw out that way so that it is nice and even in the thawing process. If you are in more of a hurry, it is fine to place them in the microwave to thaw as long as you cook them up right after they are done.

If you are planning on taking the meat that you have frozen and breading it up before cooking, you will have to let it thaw at least a little bit within the refrigerator before starting. This will make it much easier to handle. In addition to this, if you are planning on stuffing any of the poultry that you are using, you will need to make sure that you thaw it out completely, using one of the methods listed above, in order to be sure that you are safe.

It is even possible to freeze up things such as cream, cheese, milk, eggs, and butter. When you are ready to use them, there are several methods that you can use. For everything except the cream you will need to place it into the refrigerator and once it is done thawing you can use it the same as you would the fresh products. For the cream, it will also need to be thawed in the refrigerator but you will need to make sure that it is blended or mixed up a little bit during the process.

Chapter 3 – Drying

Drying is another method that you can choose to use if you would like to properly preserve your food. This is actually the oldest of the methods that has been used for preserving food. Some of the first things that were preserved include meats, grapes, currants, apples, and corn. When compared with some of the other methods for food preservation that are available, this is one of the easiest and often you will own much of the necessary equipment without even knowing it. When you dry out the food, you are taking out the moisture which helps it to keep well while you are storing it.

This method become very popular when people where traveling around. If you were traveling over the old west, you would not be able to carry food all around with you and if you have caught a deer or other animal, you would not want the food to go to waste. You might have no idea how long it will be before you can find more food so it is important to find a method that makes it easy to store the food without it going bad in the near future. Drying is the perfect method that can be used to meet these needs.

While the drying process can be really effective for many different types of food products, such as fruits and meat, it will never be able to replace some of the other methods of food preservation such as freezing and canning. This is because those methods are much better at keeping the nutrition, appearance, and the taste of the food that you are preserving. Even with this fact, drying is a good way to keep the foods that you want to enjoy preserved for a long time and adds in some variety with your meals. Some of them, such as jerky, are great snacks. One of the reasons that people love drying their foods is because these types of foods are much easier to store than some of the other preservation methods.

While there will be certain methods and rules that will be in place for commercial drying practices, there are not any rules that are in place for the method that you do so at home. There are various methods that you will be able to utilize in your own home in order to dry out the food and keep it preserved for longer. For example, you might be able to leave the food out in the sun if you can find a day that is dry and hot enough along with having enough room to keep the food out. It is even possible to do these processes with a dryer or oven as long as the climate around it is humid.

The process of drying food has gained a lot of popularity in recent years because buying the foods dried at the store has become so expensive. The drying process is pretty easy to do so many people have decided that it is worth their time to just do the process themselves. It is important to remember that while the process is not considered difficult, it will take you a lot of time and attention to get it done. Even with all of the methods that are available for drying, you will be able to use pretty much the same guidelines for all of them.

One method of drying from home that has become really popular is solar drying. This is because it is so inexpensive and needs the least amount of equipment out of all the methods. You will need to have the temperature outside be at least 95 degrees for up to 5 days in a row. The humidity must also be pretty low. This means that you will only be able to try out this method of drying in certain places. Florida and some places in the south that get very warm but do not have that much humidity are ideal for this process. On the other hand, Minnesota is probably not the place that you will be able to do this because it rarely gets that warm much less stays that warm long enough for the process.

There is still the option of drying the food while using the oven in your home, although this method will be much more expensive than some other methods of food preservation. It has been found that using an electric oven will also cost up to twelve times more than just canning the food is. You might also be interested in purchasing a food dehydrator because they can be less expensive than other methods, but you will only be able to use them for a short time throughout the year so you will need to get all of your drying done quickly.

The best method that you can use for drying is a convection oven as long as you chose the proper model. If you can find convection oven that you will be able to control the temperature to at least 120 degrees and let it continuously run rather than be controlled from a timer, you have found the perfect tool for the dehydration process. The best part is, once the drying season is over, you will be able to keep using the convection oven like a tabletop oven.

There are a few guidelines that you will have to keep in mind, regardless of the method that you choose to use for the drying out process. The first topic will be about speed. You will not be able to keep the fruits and vegetables that you want to dry sitting around for a long time before starting the process. Even if you are not going to dry them that day or the next, you should start to get them prepared as soon as you can once they have been harvested. This means that you should lay them out for drying, cool them, or blanch them right away.

The drying process itself should happen pretty quickly. You do not want the moisture to sit around in the produce or they can become bad. Keep in mind that it should be a nice even drying. You want to make sure that all of the moisture stuck inside the produce will have the chance for evaporation before the outsides start to become hard.

Once you start the drying process, you must not let the process be interrupted by anything. In addition to this, once the drying process begins, you should never let any of the food cool down during any part of the process and then start drying it again later. Mold, bacteria, and many other organisms will flourish on the food that is partly dried and that kind of defeats the purpose of doing the drying process.

You will also need to make sure to keep the temperatures right during this drying process. During the beginning of the process, it is fine if the temperature of the air around the product is relatively high. This means that you can keep the temperatures somewhere between 150 to 1 60 degrees. This allows the moister to evaporate very fast out of the food. Since the food is losing its heat during this fast evaporation, it is fine to keep the temperature high without having to worry about the increase with the foods temperature.

Once the outside of the food begins to start feeling dry and all of the surface moisture is gone, the evaporation rate will begin to slow down. This means that the food will begin to warm up and the temperature of the air around it will need to be reduced. You will need to change the temperature to somewhere near 140 degrees.

The next section will be the end of the whole process. You will find that it is more likely for the food to get scorched really easily in this process so it will be important for you to watch the food carefully. Each of the products that you might try the drying out process will need to stay below a certain temperature or else it will start to taste scorched. You might have to find a recipe in order to determine how high you will need to keep the temperatures at. A good rule of thumb is to keep the temperature high enough so that it is still taking moisture out of the food, but you do not want the temperatures to be so high that you have begun to have the food cooked.

Another thing that you will need to keep in mind is the amount of ventilation and humidity that you will need in order to accomplish this process successfully. You will want to see a rapid dehydration process happen when you are trying to dry out the products. This will usually happen when you keep the temperatures high and the humidity low around the products. If you happen to have a ton of humidity around the products, you will see that the evaporation process will slow down quite a bit.

You must keep the humidity low if you want to successfully dry out your food products. If the drying process happens to fast, you will have a problem with the outside looking like it is overdone while there is still moisture to be found in the inside. When the outside becomes hard, it will not let any moisture from inside escape and the whole process will not be able to continue on.

You will also need to make sure that the ventilation is good in your method of drying. If the moisture is not able to escape the food and evaporate with the air, it will not be able to dry out. If the air becomes trapped within the cooking method, the air will soon have more moisture than it is able to hold and you will find that the drying process will not be happening any longer. For the best results when you are going through the drying process, make sure to have good ventilation all around the oven or food dryer that you are using.

Finally, you will have to worry about getting the food to all dry evenly. This will take some extra attention and effort to accomplish but it can be done. You will need to make sure to stir around the food pieces quite a bit and even shift the racks around in the dryer or oven. This is important too because the heat will not be the same throughout the whole dryer or oven. You will also need to make sure that you do not throw too many pieces on each rack of the dryer. Make the layers thin and spread them out so that they have plenty of room to dry out.

There are plenty of great nutrients that you are able to get out of the dried fruits, vegetables, and other products that you choose to dry out. The dried fruits that you consume will be an excellent source for energy because they will have the fruit sugars in a concentrated form. Some of the vitamins and minerals that are found in the vitamins might be destroyed in the process, such as vitamin C and A. You might be able to keep some of these vitamins in if you expose the fruit to some sulfur ahead of time. These dried fruits will also contain high amounts of iron and riboflavin.

Dried vegetables will also contain a ton of great minerals and nutrients that you need to stay healthy. Some of the nutrients that you can find in the vegetables include niacin, riboflavin, and many B vitamins. Along with the fruits, both products will provide you with the fiber you need to stay strong and healthy.

Make sure to keep the water that you might use if you are cooking or soaking up the dried produce. This water will have many of the nutrients that are found in the produce and you will be able to use them in gravies, sauces, and even soups later on.

You might be wondering what types of food you will be able to dry successfully. There are many different types of fish, meat, herbs, vegetables, and fruits that you can put through the drying process. It is important to note that if you never went through the drying process before, you might want to start out small to see how successful you are. It is much easier to ruin a really small batch of food than a really large one that you have spent days on. Doing the small batch first gives you the opportunity to not only try out the drying process but to see how you enjoy the texture and taste of the dried foods that you have made.

As you get used to the whole drying process, you will notice that it is much easier to dry out fruit than it is to dry out the vegetables. Fruits will not need as much of their moisture evaporated in order to keep and get through the whole drying process. If you are trying to determine which types of fruits you should put through the drying process you might want to consider pears, apricots, peaches, cherries, berries, and apples.

There are also some vegetables that are pretty practical to dry up. These might include green beans, onions, okra, zucchini, peppers, corn, and peas. It is best if you are able to get these products from your own garden rather than from the store because the store bought versions are much more expensive along with not being as fresh as is needed for the drying process. Also, you will have to realize that it is not worth your time to dry out some types of vegetables. For example, carrots are able to be kept in a dry and cool place for many months so it would not be worth your time to try and dry these out.

Herbs are a great thing to put through the drying process and pretty much all types of them will be good for the drying process. The blossoms, seeds, and leaves are usually the best parts of the herb to dry out, although you might be able to dry out some other parts.

Lean meats are also an excellent food product to dry out in the form of jerky. You can even dry up many different types of fish as long as it is done right. There are a few types of food that are not really that great for the drying processes because they just come with too much moisture in them. Some examples of foods that are not able to dry very well include cucumbers, melons, and lettuce.

When you are becoming interested in starting the drying process, you will be able to find a large variety of hints and suggestions that you should try for the amount of time, the temperatures, and the dry method as a whole. This process will not be quite as precise as some of the other methods, such as freezing and canning, because there will be many more factors that are involved. It might take you a couple of tries to find a method that works the best for you. This is why you should start out with a small batch so that you are not ruining a whole big batch at once. It does not matter which method you choose to use, as long as enough of the moisture is removed in order to avoid spoilage in the final product.

There are a few things that you should keep in mind when you are trying to dry out food products. The first thing is that sanitation and cleanliness in the area where you are trying to dry out the foods is very essential. Along with that, you will notice that the flavoring of the dried vegetables and fruits will differ from any of the other ways that you can purchase the products such as frozen, canned or fresh. This is part of the appeal to some people. They like having the different taste added to their meals and snacks.

Methods for Drying

There are many different methods that you can choose to go about the drying process. It will often depend on what you have available and might even depend on the part of the country that you live in. Those in the south might have the conditions favorable to doing the drying process outside on some occasions while others, like those who live in the north, will never have the opportunity. This section will help to explain the different methods that are available for drying out food in order to preserve it.

The first method that you can use for the drying process is oven drying. This is often the simplest method to use when drying out your food because there is hardly any special equipment and you do not have to wait for the weather to get just right. This method is also a lot simpler and faster than using sun drying or food dryers to do the process. The one main problem that might arise from this method is that it is only able to dry a little bit of food at a time. You will not be able to come in and dry a whole animal at the same time because there just is not enough room in the oven. Most ovens will be able to hold up to 6 pounds of the food at a time.

To start out on this process, you will want to make sure that you have set your oven to the lowest setting possible. Preheat it at this setting to about 140 degrees. Make sure that when you are choosing the settings you do not pick the broiler unit part of it. If you do, the food on the top will dry up too quickly and not taste as good while the bottom food will take much longer.

Throughout the process, you will want to keep the oven somewhere between 140 degrees and 160 degrees. You might have to put a thermometer in place to help make sure the temperatures are staying right. You will place the thermometer about halfway in the middle of the top tray so that it is really easy to see. Make sure to keep checking this thermometer every half an hour or so.

You will be able to around up to two pounds of the food that you have prepared on every tray in one single layer. You can then take these trays and place them on an oven rack. You will want to make sure to allow some room, about 1 ½ inches, around each of the trays so that there is plenty of room for the air to circulate all over the place. While it is possible to stack a few trays on top of each other, it is best if you only do a couple of trays at a time with this method. When you have less food in the oven, it will dry much faster than if you are trying to do a huge batch.

You will want to make sure to keep open the oven door all throughout the drying process. This will allow the moist air to get out of the oven so that the food dries. You can use a hot pad, some wood, or even some newspaper to keep them open. You will need to leave somewhere between 4 and 6 inches open for your electric oven and about 2 inches if you have a gas oven. You can use your thermometer again here to make sure that the oven temperature is staying at the required 140 degrees.

During the whole process, you will need to make sure to rotate around the trays so that you can get some even drying. The temperatures that are found in your oven will not be the same all throughout. You will need to take the time to move the trays all around. Move them from bottom to top and from back to front at least every 30 minutes. You might need to find a method of numbering the trays so that you can have better luck with keeping them in order every time that you move them around. If you are using this method to dry out vegetables and fruits, you will need to make sure to stir them around while you are rotating as well. The jerky that you are making will need turned over every once in a while so that it will not stick on the trays.

Another method that you might use for food drying is a food dryer. These are nice to use because they will control all of the ventilation and heat needs that you have. It is not often that you will need to use one of these in your own home because most of the time you will dry smaller quantities of food and these food dryers will work with large food quantities. This is why you will usually find these in commercial use although it is fine for you to use one in your own home if you wish.

One benefit of using a food dryer is that it will take up less electricity than your electric oven will for doing the same process for the same food amounts. It is important to note that the temperatures found in food dryers will be a little lower than those found in your electric oven, usually around 120 degrees. This means that the drying process will take longer using this method that with you oven.

There are many places where you are able purchase a food drying. Some of them include stores for health foods, farm supply stores, and even hardware stores. The amount that you pay for a food dryer will often vary depending on the special features that come on them, the heating element that it uses, and the size of the food dryer. Take the time to look around to find the right food dryer to meet your needs.

Before using the food dryer, you will want to make sure to preheat it all up. Make sure the internal temperature is 125 degrees. Take out the trays and then pace whatever food you are drying on top of them before stacking the trays inside the dryer. Once you have placed all of the trays inside, you will want to raise the temperature up to about 140 degrees. Using this method, it could take anywhere from 4 to 12 hours in order to dry the vegetables and fruits in the food dryer. Make sure to read the directions in your recipe and in the food dryer to ensure that you are keeping them in for the right amount of time.

You should never use any space heaters in order to dry your food. These will simply stir up a lot of dirt and dust ad will simply contaminates the food which you are trying to preserve. Along with this, you should never dry out the food using clothes dryer or a furnace vent. Just stick with the dryers and other methods that are specifically meant for drying your food.

The next option that you can choose for drying your food is to use sun drying. This method is the way that it was done in the past before there were the options of using an oven or other special dryer. You are able to dry out your food by using the sun and the heat that it makes in order to dry out the food. You will have to realize that one nice day will not be enough to properly dry out your food. You will need to find a few nice days in a row, a bright sun, some really low humidity, and temperatures that fall somewhere near 100 degrees. This is not possible in most parts of the country which is why most people do not choose to use this method.

There will be a lot of attention and work that will go in to using this method, you will have to make sure that the weather stays nice, that it gets covered up at night, and that there are no insects that are attacking the food. You will also not be able to do this method if the air around you is not very clean and you live right beside a road that is busy. As you can see, there are not very many circumstances where you will be able to do this method.

If you are still determined to use this method for drying out your food, you might find it very beneficial to get a container that will be able to help you out. There are certain types that will aid in catching all of the heat that is from the sun and keeping it near the food. This will really help to speed up the drying process. In addition to this, these kinds of containers will also help to protect the food that you leave outside from birds and insects.

When you are using one of these containers, you will want to start out by placing some of the food on the trays and cover them up with some sort of netting. This netting will help you to keep the dust, and insects away from the food. Once you are ready, you can take the dryer container and place it directly in the sunlight somewhere up high so that it will stay away from animals and other harmful things. At the end of the process, you will want to remove the product from the sun and place it in a shady place. This will help to keep it from scorching towards the end and yet it will still continue to dry.

If you live in an area that gets warm during the day and cool during the night, you will want to bring your dryer inside during the night. Any dew that might form along with sudden changes in temperatures will put the moisture back to your foods and the drying time will dramatically increase.

When you are using this method, you will find that it will often take days to accomplish. Vegetables and fruits take up to 7 days to completely dry up with the sun. You will find that each method is different and will often depend both on the food type and the conditions in the atmosphere.

Fruit Drying

One of the foods that you might be interested in drying is fruit. You will need to make sure that the fruit that you are using is of good quality so that it will not spoil or get bad during the whole process. You will want to select some fruit that has fully ripened and is fresh. Basically, do not pick any fruit that you would not already be keeping on your own table.

After you have chosen the fruit that you want to use, you will have to go through and sort it all out before washing it all thoroughly. After the fruit has been washed, you can make sure to cut off any overripe or bruised pieces and discard them. If you leave any of the bad pieces on the fruit, you might find that your whole batch will have a bad flavor to it. It is better to go through and cut of all the bad pieces, even ones that you would normally eat, in order to ensure that you get the best product possible when drying. You must also make sure that you use the proper handling processes during the whole thing in order to keep the fruit properly preserved.

Every fruit that you will be drying out with have to go through some kind of treatment before you get started. This is not as bad as it sounds. For example, if you are going to dry up some apples you will need to slice, core, and peel them before they can be dried. If the fruits have a pit in them, like apricots and peaches, you will need to halve them up and pit them. Make sure that when you are cutting up the fruit you take the time to make the pieces as uniform as possible. This will allow them to dry much more evenly. Thin pieces will dry much faster than the thick ones so keep this in mind when cutting up your fruit.

There are some fruits that will have a tough skin that is almost wax-like. You will need to take the time to crack these skins so that the coating can be removed. When you remove the wax like coating, you are allowing the moisture that is inside the fruit to come up near the surface and evaporate during the drying process. Some fruits that you might have to do this process with include plums, grapes, cherries, and blueberries. You will not see as good of results if you just start to dry the fruits without first cracking the skins.

In order to crack the skin off the fruit, you will have to place the fruit in with some boiling water. Get the water all boiling hot and leave the fruit inside it for up to 60 seconds. At this time you will take the fruit out of the boiling water and dip it in to some cold water. Drain them with some towels and then take the skin off.

It is also possible to do this process with some lye solutions, but you should proceed with caution with these things. It can get dangerous when handling the lye solutions so make sure to know exactly what you are doing before starting.

You will have to take some precautions with light colored foods as well. Many fruits, such as apricots, pears, peaches, and apples, will start to turn brown shortly after they become exposed to air around them through the cutting process. This browning process is usually caused when a chemical change, oxidation, begins to occur. If you do not take the right precautions to stop the oxidation process, you will ruin the appearance, aroma, flavor, and texture of each fruit you are trying to dry.

The best method that you can use to prevent this process is to cover the fruits with an antioxidant. The right one will be able to prevent your fruit from turning brown. Take a little bit of ascorbic acid and mix it in with some water. Sprinkle this whole mixture on top of the fruit as you go to stop the oxidation process right away. You will be able to purchase the ascorbic acid through most of the drugstores near you.

You should not let your fruit soak in vinegar water or salt. This is because both of these methods will add more water into the fruit which will in turn make the drying process and time much longer. On top of this, using a soaking method will take out many of the vitamins and other nutrients from the fruits making them much less healthy for you to consume.

One thing to keep in mind about using the ascorbic acid to coat your fruits is that it will only last for a short time. You will need to take the time to do some other forms of treatment before starting the drying process with your fruits.

Using sulfur is one of the best things that you can do in order to preserve the color of your fruit. If you do not use a method that is permanent, you will find that your apples and other fruits that are light will start turning dark throughout the whole drying process and in to the storage time. In addition to being a great tool to use in order to prevent the oxidation process, sulfur will also help you to keep the vitamins C and A in the fruit during the process itself. While sulfur is not considered a preservative, it is often used because it will discourage the microbes and insects that try to get into the food and cause spoilage.

Sulfur will not cause any harm to the fruits that you are using it on nor will you have to worry about consuming the products later one when you use sulfur. Sulfur is actually one of the minerals that often occurs in the foods that you eat naturally and is something that is necessary for life to go on. The sulfur that you use during this process will become an acid when mixed in with the water found in your fruit, but it evaporates really easily during the drying phase. There will be a slight residue that is left on the fruits, but it is harmless and your body will easily be able to excrete it later on.

In order for the sulfur to be the most effective, you will want to put it on your fruits right after you have prepared it. There are a few methods that you can use in order to expose the fruit to the sulfur and each of them will have positives and negatives to consider. The first method is using sulfur fumes and the second one is to use a sulfite solution.

To start with are the sulfur fumes. This method is often considered to be more effective compared to the sulfur solutions, but you will often need more equipment and time in order to make this method word. Some of the equipment that you will need includes a box that contains some screens and trays along with some cheesecloth to cover it all up.

The time with which you will need to put the sulfur on each fruit will vary depending on the type of fruit that you are dealing with. You might have to check with the recipe that you are using to find the time that works the best. You should also keep in mind that if you use sulfur fumes on your fruits, you should do the drying process outside of the house. This is because the sulfur fumes will often leave a very unpleasant odor that would not be good in your home. You must also be extra careful with the fumes. You will find that they can be very irritating for your nose and eyes.

Often people will choose to soak their fruit in the sulfite solution. This method is pretty easy to do and does not need as many materials in order to complete. You should keep in mind that this method will not be as effective as using the sulfur fumes but it will work just fine for basic home drying needs.

When using the sulfite solution method, you will need to add on some time to your drying process. This is because there is some soaking involved so the fruit will have extra moisture that needs to be gotten rid of. You can dry fruit that has been put in a sulfite solution inside the house or outside, it is all up to you.

If you do not feel comfortable with using sulfur with your foods, you can always choose to use steam blanching. It is a good alternative although it will not be nearly as effective. There will be a lot of vitamins that are lost through this method and the whole process will take much longer. This method is usually not recommended unless it is the only method available.

After you have gotten done with preparing all of the fruits, it is time to go through the drying process. You will want to set out some sheets and arrange the fruit all along the sheet. Make sure to keep them in one single layer for the best results when drying. Once the trays are filled up, you will want to place them into the dryer or the oven. Make sure to leave some room between the trays to ensure that they are getting the air all around them.

If you are using the oven to dry out your fruit, you will need to remember that the door will need to be left open a little bit. If you have the option of using an electric fan, you can place it right in front so that it can help the oven go faster with the drying process. If you are using a dryer to do this process, you will not need to worry about leaving it open or anything. The dryer will take care of all the ventilation and other things that you need.

There will be several factors to take into account when determining how long to dry the fruits for. Mostly it will all depend on the amount of fruit that you are drying all at once and how big the pieces are. For example, thin slices of apples and grapes can usually be done in about 6 hours while large fruits with lots of juice will take 10 hours. If you are unsure about whether the fruit is done you can take a piece out and cut it up. You should not be able to get any moisture out of the fruit when it is done.

If the drying process sounds like something that you would like to do, here are a few recipes that you should try out for your first time.

Apple Rings With Sugar

1 lb. apple
1 c water
2 Tbsp. lemon juice
1 Tbsp. cinnamon

Take the apples and slice them up into rings that are not lager than ¼ inch thick. Sprinkle on the cinnamon before placing into the dehydrator. Let them sit in the oven or the dryer for up to 10 hours at temperatures of 135 degrees. They will be crisp and leathery in texture when they are done. If you want the rings to be whiter, you can soak them in the lemon juice and water beforehand. Make sure to take some paper towels and pat them dry before putting into the dehydrator to speed up the process. Double or triple the ingredients to fit your needs

Banana Honey Chips

1 lb. bananas
¼ c. lemon juice
¼ c. honey

Take the bananas and make sure to slice them into medallions. Dip them in with a mixture of lemon juice and honey. Make sure to pat them dry using some paper towels before placing into the dehydrator. You will leave them in the oven or dryer for up to 20 hours or until done at a temperature of 135 degrees. If you would like crispier chips, you should choose green bananas to start with. On the other hand, if you would like some chips that are sweeter, you can choose ripe bananas.
Vegetable Drying

The next type of food that you may be interested in drying is vegetables. You might be surprised at how many vegetables you can actually dry by yourself at home. Much like with drying out the fruits, you will want to make sure that you pick out vegetables that are mature and fresh. If you pick out old products just because they are cheaper or for some other reason, you will be really disappointed in the taste and the end result of your drying products. You should also make sure that you do not buy too many vegetables. Just purchase a few pounds worth or enough to dry all at once. Purchasing too much can mean that there are leftovers that might be too old by the time that you are ready to use them next.

After you have picked out the vegetables that you are going to use, it is best to wash them in order to get all the dirt off and then cut out the bad spots that are left on them. After the vegetables are prepared, you can cut them into small pieces for the drying process. Remember that the smaller pieces will dry much faster than the ones that are thick or bigger.

Before you place the vegetables into the dryer or oven, you are most likely going to have to blanch them first. Consult with your recipe first but most of the vegetables that you use will need to undergo this process. In order to do the blanching process, you will need to place the vegetables into some boiling water for a little bit before you allow them to dry.

Blanching is a very important process that you need to go through ahead of time. With vegetables, the drying process is not able to stop the enzymes from working, while the blanching process is able to do this. You will need to get these enzymes to stop or else the flavor and the color of your vegetables will be ruined during the drying and the storage process. There are a few types of vegetables that do not need to be blanched. These will include onions, okra, and mushrooms.

In addition to this, blanching will be able to assist in protecting certain nutrients that are in the vegetables. Your dried vegetables will be much healthier if you put them through this blanching process compared to leaving it out. You will be able to also reduce down the drying time a little bit as well. It is important to note that a few nutrients might be lost in the blanching process because water is used.

There is the option of using steam blanching, but it often takes up more time. The good news is that there are fewer nutrients that will be lost in the process. You will have to find the right balance between blanching too little and not deactivating the enzymes and blanching too long and losing a lot of great nutrients.

In order to blanch, you will need to place the cut up vegetable pieces into some water and let it boil. After the time is up according to your recipe, you will need to take it out and place the vegetables in some ice water. Drain it all out and then pat it dry with some paper towels in order to get rid of any extra moisture. Make sure to save all of the water to use later. This water is often great when added to gravies, stews, and soups because it will add a lot of nutrients and flavor to these dishes.

After you have finished preparing the vegetables, it is time to start the drying process. You can do much like with the vegetables and lay out some trays. Make sure to arrange the vegetables on the trays so that they are in one layer all around. After the trays are all full, you can stack them into the dryer or the oven, making sure to let a little space be available between and around all of the trays to allow the air to go all around them. Placing the trays too close will make the drying process take much longer.

When using the oven, you will want to make sure that the oven is left open a little bit in order to allow all the air to get out. You might find a fan is useful in this process and might speed it all up. If you are using your food dryer, you will not have to worry about the ventilation at all. You will want to make sure that the temperatures for the vegetables stay around 140 degrees at all times.

During the drying process, you will need to make sure to stir around the vegetable pieces at least once every 30 minutes. This allows both sides to get exposed to the air during the process. You will also need to take the time to move the trays around on the rack so that they are all cooked evenly.

Most of the vegetables that you will be drying will take up to 12 hours to cook. You will need to consult your recipe to ensure that you are giving them the proper amount of time to dry. It often depends on the temperature at which they are drying, the method that you are using, and how much you are trying to dry. When the vegetables are done they will be brittle and hard. You will be able to hit a piece with your hammer and it will shatter when they are sufficiently dry.

There are some vegetables that you will have to take extra precautions with when drying and even some that are best preserved and stored in methods other than drying. For example, vegetables such as potatoes, rutabagas, parsnips, turnips, and carrots often do much better being stored in their original form rather than going through the drying process. You are even able to keep them for several months down in the basement without having to do anything to them.

Some other vegetables, such as asparagus and broccoli do much better being frozen compared to dry because the freezing will help them to keep their fresh texture and flavor. Drying will often take a lot of that away from these vegetables.

It is possible to dry a combination of different vegetables together if you wish. You will just have to remember that each of the vegetables that you are drying will have different times that it will take to dry. This means that some will dry more quickly than others so you will have to watch the clock and pull them out in time. If any of the vegetables that you are drying have strong odors, you should not have them drying with any other vegetables. This is because the other vegetables will absorb odor that is strong and their flavor will change.

Any vegetables that you are drying for a salad should be done so separately, but they are able to be mixed up and stored with each other in a type of blend. Some of the vegetables that you might want to consider for your salad include parsley, green peppers, spinach, onion, celery, tomatoes, and carrots.

As with the salad ingredients, any vegetables that you will be using for a soup should also have different drying period. This will allow you the options to mix and match the vegetables in various ways to work with your needs. If you dry them all together, you will be stuck with just having one use of the vegetables because they are all sharing the same flavors.

There are many different ways that you are able to use the dried vegetables. When you are ready to use the vegetables again, you will need to soak them for a bit in order to get them ready to eat again and to save some time on the whole cooking process. You will need to take 1 cup of the vegetables and place them in about 2 cups of the water. These need to soak for around 2 hours. If the water is almost gone before the time runs out, you will need to add in some more. When the vegetables are done you will notice that they look almost like they originally did. You can use these in soups, casseroles, and any other dish that you would like.

The following recipes are meant to help you get on the right track for finding uses of your dried vegetables when you are ready to use them.

Vegetable soup

3 c. dried vegetables, mixed
1 c. meat, diced
Pepper
Salt

Cover up the vegetables with some boiling water and then allow them to soak for about 1 hour. After the hour is done, you can allow them to simmer for another 2 hours so that they become tender. After the vegetables are all ready, you can add in the meat and the seasonings to taste. It is fine to mix in some other vegetables with the mixed ones if you do not have the right types.

Creamed Corn

4 c. water, boiling
1 c. corn, dried
½ c. milk
1 Tbsp. flour
2 tsp. sugar
1 Tbsp. butter
Pepper
Salt

Take the corn and add it into the water. Let it stand for around 30 minutes before letting it go down to a simmer. The corn will need to simmer for an hour or until the corn becomes tender. Drain out the water before adding in the rest of the ingredients. Let it all simmer for 5 minutes longer, making sure to stir the whole mixture along so that it does not scorch.

Herb Drying

When you want to preserve herbs, you will find that drying is the best method that you can use. Most of the other methods just do not seem to work at well with the small leaves so it is best if you use this method. It is pretty easy to go about drying herbs and it usually will not take too long for it to happen since most herbs are pretty small and do not contain much moisture in them to start with. You will simply need to expose the seeds, flowers, or the leaves to the warm air either in your oven of in a dryer. Leave them in until all the moisture as evaporated.

One thing about drying out herbs, it is not really recommended that you use sun drying with the herbs. While it might work out well with other forms of foods, you will find that the herbs will lose their color and flavor when using this method.

If you are harvesting the herbs, you will need to make sure to get them right before you start to see the flowers open for the first stage. Get them in the early morning. This is so that the dew is all gone and will not keep them wet but also avoids the wilting process. You will want to make sure that the leaves do not become bruised and that you do not leave anything laying out in the sun after you are done with the harvesting. As with the other forms of products that you are drying, you will want to make sure to rinse off the herb using some cool water and then gently shake them in order to remove the extra moisture from cleaning them. Make sure to get rid of all the imperfect leaves and stems along with anything that is soiled or bruised.

Using a dryer or dehydrator will be the easiest and fastest method to drying up all of the herbs because you will be able to control the exact circulation of the air along with the temperature. If you are using this method, you will want to let it preheat to no less than 95 degrees. If you live in an area that has high humidity, you might find that you will need a higher temperature such as 125 degrees to accomplish the same goal. When you are ready, you can place the herbs onto the trays for the dryer in one layer. The drying process will usually take between 1 and 4 hours to complete, but you should make sure to check on them every once in a while so that they do not get overdone.

You will know that the herbs are done when they begin to crumble and also when the stems begin to break once you bend them. You might have to check with the instructions on your dryer to ensure that you are doing it for the correct amount of time.

There are many different types of herbs that you can do. The first type is the kind that is known as less tender. These are the ones that are really sturdy such as parsley, thyme, sage, and rosemary and they are usually easier to dry up if you do not use a dehydrator. Instead, you will be able to tie them up into bundles and then just hang them up to dry out with the air.

The second type of herbs that you can use is known as tender leaf. These might include mint, lemon balm, tarragon, oregano, and basil. These all contain a high level of moisture and you will find that they mold very easily if they do not dry up quickly. You might want to try and hang up these herbs in some paper bags and allow them to dry for a little bit. Often you will need to punch in some holes in the bag and then close up the top with some rubber bands. You will need to place these bags somewhere that have a lot of air currents to circulate through and get rid of the moisture.

Using a microwave is also a method that you can consider because it is pretty fast and easy to do. Make sure to only use this method if you are preparing small quantities and to read any of the directions that come along with the microwave to ensure that you are doing it right.

No matter which method you are choosing in order to dry out the herbs, you will be able to tell that they are ready once they crumple up and feel crispy dry. You can package and store them up at this time it is possible to leave the leaves either whole like they are or crumple them up before you put them into storage. All herbs should be put within some airtight containers and left in a dry, cool, and dark area in order to maintain their original fragrance and color.

One thing to keep in mind about herbs is that they are usually stronger in the dried form than in the fresh form. Sometimes this difference can be up to 4 times more. If you are substituting in the dried herbs for a recipe, you will need to alter the recipe accordingly.

The following are some recipes that you can use for drying out a few herbs that you might be interested in.

Drying Chives

Take the chives and cut off any of the stems that are old or have bad spots on them. These can alter the flavor of the rest of the leaves if mixed together. Turn on the dehydrator and let the internal temperature get to about 100 degrees. Let the chives cook for a couple of hours or until crispy and crumbly. The drying process might take longer if you are doing a larger batch of the chives. Once it is done you can store it up in some containers that do not let in any air and keep them out of the light.

Drying Dill

Take the seeds and the leaves and spread them out on a tray and allow to air dry for a bit. You will not want to use a dryer if you can help it because this might mess with the oils that are in this leaf. When the leaves and seeds are done, you can place them into some containers and keep them air tight. Make sure not to use any paper bags for this or else the herbs will lose their oils. Store the dill somewhere that is dark and dry. A cabinet will do just fine.

Meat Drying

Finally, it is also possible to dry and preserve is various types of meat. In fact, this used to be the only method that was available to making sure that the meat was preserved for a long time. Even those who first came to America chose to dry up the meat that they took with them because it just was not feasible to take enough fresh meat with them when they came from Europe or even across the country. If they had tried to bring the fresh meat around with them, it would have all spoiled and they would not have been able to survive on the food that they had. Turning the meat into jerky helped it to last a lot longer so that they could get to their destination without worrying about having the right amount of foods that they needed.

Jerky has been popular for many years because it is an easy form of preserving the meat that you need for a long time. While many people do not need to preserve the meat as much anymore since it is readily available, there are still many uses for it. Often jerky is a very popular snack for those who are out camping or hiking or even something nice to keep around the house. Purchasing dried jerky at the store can get really expensive and you might find that it is actually a whole lot cheaper to just make the jerky in your own home rather than go and try to purchase it at the store.

You can still find forms of dried meat, although it is usually called jerky now. Instead of using the old method of laying it out in the sun to dry up, most of the time jerky will be made using your oven.

Jerky has become a really popular snack and you will be able to find it all around including gas stations and grocery stores. While there really doesn't have to be any special reason to enjoy jerky, it is really popular among hunters, hikers, and campers because it will keep for a while, is light in weight, and is compact.

Some people do not see the point of taking the time to dry up the meat that they are going to consume. They figure that there is plenty of fresh meat available to them so it is just a waste of their time to make other forms of meat to preserve. But many people find it a lot of fun and a great way to make a delicious snack at home. Another positive is that when you make your own jerky, it is about half the price of going to the store and purchasing the same amount.

When you are ready to start making your own jerky at home, it is time to get ready and prepare the meat. You are able to use pretty much any of the lean meats that you want for this process. Most people will choose to use venison and beef during this process although it is also fine to use poultry and fish. The important thing is that you choose lean and fresh meats and that you make sure to cut off the connective tissue and fat that is left on them. These can spoil the meat that you are drying so it is best if you take the off.

You can decide to let the meat freeze a little bit in order to get it to cut up more easily. You should slice along the grain and make long and even strips that are thin. Doing it this way will help to make the jerky less brittle and chewier. The thinner you can make the slices the quicker they will be able to dry.

If you are using any meat from wild game in this process you should make sure to let it stay frozen for a minimum of 30 days. This will help you to kill off any parasite larvae that might be left on them and keep you from getting an infection of trichinosis.

There are two methods that you can use for drying the meat. You can either choose to dry it up how it is or season it with seasonings or sauces to meet your tastes. For the most basic ingredients most people will use pepper and salt. During the drying process, you will be using the salt more as a type of seasoning instead of a preservative. This means that you will need to set the internal temperature of the dryer to 140 degrees to make sure that no spoilage occurs throughout the drying. Do not put on too many seasonings or you will not be able to taste the flavor in the meat.

If you are going to season the meat before drying it, you should place it into a bowl or a pan and let it be covered up overnight with the seasonings. The same thing will happen if you are trying to marinate the meat as well. This will help make sure that the meat has time to catch all of the seasonings during the night before you place it in the dryer and cook it all up.

The following are some recipes that you can try out if you are interested in making some jerky in your own home.

Jerky Recipe

2 lbs. ground meat
2 Tbsp. olive oil
2 Tbsp. seasoning (no salt)

Take the ground meat and cut it up before mixing it with a tiny bit of the olive oil and some of the seasonings. Make sure that the seasoning that you use in this recipe does not contain salt in it. Spread out the meat on the dryer and then let them cook until done at 125 degrees. These will be able to be stored for a month or more once they are done.

Marinade for Jerky

1 c. ketchup
¼ c. sugar, brown
½ c. vinegar
3 Tbsp. Worcestershire Sauce
Salt

2 tsp. mustard, dry
Pepper

Take all of these ingredients and mix them together in a bowl and set aside. Next you can take the meat that you are using for jerky and cut it up into the strips that you want. Place the jerky into the bowl and let it marinate overnight. The next day you can place them into the dryer and let go until done.

Chapter 4—Pickling

Another form of food preservation that you can use is known as pickling. This method is meant to extend the life cycle of a food by marinating that food in with a brine of some sort. The method is meant to create some lactic acid by controlling the environment using the bacteria. This mixture will result in your food being preserved through a process of fermentation.

The brine that you will be using during this process is usually created by using some form of an acid, some water, and some salt. This mixture is often heated and added in with some other spices for some more flavor. The combination of these spices is meant to prevent bacteria from growing inside so that your food stays nice and fresh over time.

A variant within the concept is visible in dishes such as kimchi and sauerkraut. Rather than brine, this method purely draws the water out of the product itself applying dry salt. The cabbage utilized in both dishes will be kept at room temperature for the desired timeframe to allow sufficient fermentation along with the creation of moisture. Both can be stored with jars or other mediums.

Pickling is highly popular in the house canning and jarring sector. The most common example could be the pickled cucumber, usually precisely what is thought of when someone identifies a pickle. Other items such as onions, garlic, peas, cauliflower, asparagus and even fish are likewise popular pickled items with both buyers and home canning enthusiasts.

Around the planet, pickling has long been used as a way of preserving food for long trips. In addition to smoking and salting foods, pickling enabled travelers to bring with them healthier foods that may be stored for a lengthy duration. Pickling became seriously popular during the ship-fairing days and nights of colonialism as well as exploration. Sailors would start for long trips throughout the vast oceans along with large quantities of pickled foods to aid in sustaining them through the voyage.

In contemporary times, pickled products possess much popularity as a food that offers special health improvements to people. Pickled foods are great for balancing the body's electrolytes. This is thanks to the natural water and salt that goes into the pickling process. Pickles are a very important thing to eat following a hard workout for example. In addition, pickled foods have major benefit of large amounts of B vitamins, which assists in digestion amongst other pursuits. This is due to the creation from the bacteria during the procedure.

Basics of Pickling

Any time summer vegetable gardens and farm stands overflow with the bounty of the season, there's no better time for you to start using the best it has to offer. While salads and various vegetable dishes springs to mind, did you ever think of preserving summer vegetables for utilization in the fall and cold months of winter?

Pickling, like canning, does require several basic cooking equipment tools that will not only make the task easier but better. You'll need a heavy-bottomed stainless or enameled pot to prepare the recipes; stay away from any aluminum items, since the lightweight aluminum will react with the acid in veggies, like tomatoes. In addition, your finished product will probably taste like the material. You'll also require a large pot or perhaps canning kettle that has a lid. This type of pot is often made from an exceptionally thin metal so the water can go to a boil easily; this pot will assist you to process the packed jars of vegetables you can be pickling.

To move the actual jars in and out from the hot water bathroom, a canning rack as well as a jar lifter can make the process much simpler. In order to prevent spilling your pickling products, it is a great idea to use a canning funnel, particularly one with a wide mouth. Finally, the jars themselves include the final piece of this puzzle. Make sure the canning jars you make use of are absolutely clean and free from chips and nicks so that nothing can get in or out of the jars that you are using. It is recommended that you avoid using processed food jars, such as mustard or mayonnaise jars. Then of course you'll need clean bands and lids. After you use the tops, you cannot reuse them again. The lids is not going to ensure a tight seal should you use them an extra time.

Produce that is pickled at its best regarding freshness will usually give you the best result. The freshest produce will also have the crispiest texture, needed for a good pickle. Vegetables that you grow in a garden make probably the most the best pickles, and growing the preserving ingredients yourself inspires an awareness of pride. If you do not have a garden, look to other places for fresh vegetables and other things to pickle, keeping away from ones with imperfections or soft regions. Fast is equally important—makes your right away after picking. Maintaining the freshness from your vegetables is key factor during the pickling process.

Salt can be an important ingredient in many pickling methods. Most brines, the salt will temper the total amount of flavors, mainly because it does this whenever you put salt on your food at meal time. In many cases, salt will draw the water away from vegetables that you are pickling, such as vegetables, to improve their texture and taste. Kosher sodium and pickling sodium, which are just about identical, usually are used as the main types to make shelf-stable pickles. Don't substitute common desk salt. Some people will add plenty of salt to their brines to achieve a pronounced flavor—but the actual subtleties of lemon, herbs, and spices can give you the same effects.

Acids are another important element in creating pickling products. Kars of pickles that have been properly sealed can stay on shelves for a while since they have the right level of acidification, meaning the pH found around the contents is stabilized, with all of the bacteria eradicated. Acid inside pickling takes a pair of forms: citric acid and vinegar. Vinegar, known as an acetic chemical p, works on the pickled produce to keep them stabilize to their right pH levels. Different types of vinegars have different examples of strength. Most vinegar that is used in pickling use a grain strength around 5 or 6 percent. Avoid vinegars with a grain strength that is lower than the menu requirements, as doing this could result with your pickles not acidify appropriately.

Citric acid will often take the form of juice via citrus: lemon, calcium, and orange. That embellishes and brightens the actual flavors that come with the pickles and also complements other materials, but it does not usually supply a acidification basis.

Heat penetration might be another aspect for acidification. Brines will get to a boil and also poured quickly straight into their jars right away before their particular temperature drops under 195°F. This takes less than two minutes. Jars remain inside boiling-water for the recommended time to make sure the temperature of everything reaches a temperature that kills any bacteria present. If the jars are sealed properly, the mixtures from the vinegar and heat will be able to reliably take care of the bacteria around the contents and everything can be safely eaten to enjoy for a long time to come.

All of the combinations of the vegetables, fruits, any vinegar and the pickling liven defines the picker's palate. But often it is the pickling spices—the special and flavorful mixture of spices and herbs included in brine—that plays probably the most special role. Different combos of all the herbs and also spices help develop pickles with special flavors, and you should make time for experimenting with your elements is how you determine how you would like your products to turn out. As you get confidence after doing it a couple of times, change up the recipes to match your tastes. Always remember to report your modifications in order that you can easily repeat the process.

Pickling spice is like barbeque sauce; everyone includes a style along with a taste preference. For a more aromatic approach, the recipe might have more than 6 or 8 spices—such as bay leaves, mustard seeds, dill, peppercorns, and whole allspice. Acquire pickling spice mixes or make your own.

Equipment Needed

There are a number of utensils it is advisable to make pickles and also relishes. One thing to keep in mind is to think of how acidic your pickles will be. If they will have a high salt content, you might want to consider getting specific jars that can keep up with it.

For fermenting, you can use a crock or jewel jar, unchipped enamel-lined pot, heavy food grade cheap container, or significant glass jar or perhaps bowl. Jars and also crocks need loose-fitting protects. Use a weighty plate or significant glass lid topped that has a weight to keep vegetables below the top of brine. A food grade cheap bag containing several 1/2 tablespoons involving salt and 3 quarts of water or perhaps a glass jar loaded with water makes a fantastic weight. Bricks or jewel weights can impart an undesirable flavor.

To temperature pickling liquids, utilize unchipped enamel ware items, stainless steel, or perhaps aluminum. Never use most things that are galvanized, or perhaps copper, brass or perhaps iron. These metals react while using acids or salts in order to cause undesirable color changes, and may possibly form harmful substances.

The pot needs to be large enough in order to simmer the materials without boiling more than and, if the recipe calls for a rolling skin boil; it should have thrice the capacity of the recipe. Use start kettles unless usually specified.

Use a boiling water bath canner to method jars after completing. Standard canning jars in good shape and new two-piece canning covers are preferred. However, mayonnaise or salad dressing jars and also new two-piece canning lids can be employed.

Miscellaneous kitchen apparatus includes: a teakettle, saucepans, spoons in order to stir and slotted spoons in order to lift, a ladle, launch, standard measures, family scale, timer, tongs for working out with jars in and beyond boiling water, bath canner and pot holders.

Pickling Olives

Using a sharp knife, complete a single deep lower lengthways in each olive to support the fermentation course of action then put them in the container with this liquid. Weigh the olives down that have a large diameter plate so they are all covered by this liquid. The plate must not fit too tightly in the container so these gasses can get away. It is not necessarily critical to exclude oxygen just as the winemaking course of action, so with this method there's no requirement to seal this container.

The olives need to be fermented at room temperature for about a month before they may be eaten, but will end up more flavorsome and also fully mature after 3 months. They can be tasted at any time during fermentation as a means of checking flavor. The bitter chemical substances are safe to nibble on.

The reason regarding fermenting the olives on this traditional way should be to break down this phenolic compounds as well as the glycoside, oleuropein which are included in the raw fruit giving them their severe bitter taste. When these compounds are broken down, lactic acid will be produced. This is a wonderful natural preservative that may enable the olives being stored without refrigeration for many months.

Aside through the fiddly, time consuming process of cutting each individual olive, this traditional way of pickling olives is reasonably straightforward and creates excellent results. The last product can always be served with numerous herbs and herbs, steeped in essential olive oil or vinegar flavored using chili, garlic or "lemon " juice or filled with peppers, cheese or perhaps anchovies. By using this traditional and not at all hard method you will never need to feel postpone pickling your unique olives again.

Drying Olives Recipe

2 kg. Olives
1 ¼ lt. water
600 ml. vinegar, white
3 Tbsp. salt
4 garlic cloves

1 Tbsp. oregano
4 red chilies
Olive oil

Take the olives and slit them on each side in order to release out the juice in it that is bitter. Let them sit in some salted water for about a week and making sure to change out the water every day. After a week you can wash them off and drain out the olives before placing them into some glass jars that are clean. Fill up a bowl with some water and add in the salt. Float 1 egg inside the bowl and when it becomes the size of a 10 cent piece, you know you have enough salt. Add in the vinegar next. Cover the olives with this mix before adding in the oregano, garlic, and chilies. Add the olive oil last and then seal. Set this aside for a month before enjoying.

Problems with Pickling

There are a lot of problems that can occur when you are using the pickling method as a form of preservation. This section is devoted to discovering some of these problems and teaching you how to avoid them.

The first problem that you might notice is bitter pickles. Bitter pickles indicate an excessive amount vinegar; check the actual recipe. Note: This can be caused by using salt substitutes. You might have to experiment a little bit to see which method works the best for you so that you are not ending up with a product that does not taste that good.

The next problem that you might notice when working on pickling is that the pickles or other product are really cloudy. Cloudy pickles really are a warning that your pickles could possibly have spoiled— especially whenever they were fresh jam-packed. The introduction associated with an airborne yeast, using metal pans, putting table salt, and using hard water during production can also have this result. If the pickled product seems greasy or smells funny, chuck it out.

You might have a problem with your pickles if they look discolored or off in any way. Discolored pickles are often the fault from the pan that you used or having hard water in your home. There is also the possibility that strong spices can bleed over directly into pickles, giving them an alternative hue.

One thing that you should keep in mind about your pickled products and the color that they are is that a blue or green tint is normal. Green-or blue-tinted garlic oil isn't cause regarding concern. It just ensures that the garlic ingested the metals with your cooking utensils or the garlic people used was fresh. It's still perfectly safe to enjoy.

Hollow cucumbers are safe to enjoy. The cucumber was too big or was hollow when canning. If your cucumber floats with water, it's pickling cucumber. The brine may also have been way too weak or way too strong.

You will also need to watch out for a pale coloring to your products. Pale coloring may perhaps mean your produce was encountered with light or was of poor quality. Make sure that you use the best products available when pickling and that you store the ingredients in a nice, cool, and dark place.

Dark coloring may be a consequence of minerals in the water. In addition, it could also be the result of overcooking, using iodized salt, or even a variety of different vinegars, such as malt vinegar. You will need to make sure that you are doing the process exactly right in order to avoid darkening of the color. If this is your first time pickling, you might want to consider doing 1 or 2 jars of it to ensure that it is done correctly before wasting a lot of time and money doing a whole batch and finding out that you have done it wrong and do not like it. If you didn't change virtually any components, darkening may perhaps indicate spoilage. Whenever in doubt, chuck it out!

Bubbly brine can be a sign that the meat has begun to spoil. Throw these kinds of pickles out right away and do not eat them or else you and your family will get really sick.

Pink pickles may result the use of overly ripe dill with your pickle blend. The actual introduction of fungus is another achievable reason. If the actual pickles are tender, the liquid over cast, or the foodstuff feels slimy, it's likely some sort of yeast problem along with the pickles should always be discarded.

Slimy pickles could be the result of a variety of causes. The volume of salt or vinegar utilized in the mix might not have been adequate, the pickles might not have been totally included in brine, the canning process might not have been used correctly, yeast was introduced, moldy spices was used, jars was improperly sealed, or the pickles was kept in too hot a space (70°F is the greatest temperature to promote proper pickling). These are generally not safe to enjoy.

Bland pickles may be a consequence of use of cucumbers which were not meant to use in pickling. Store-bought cucumbers often times have a waxy finish. The brine can't permeate this; the pickles from these cucumbers are usually less flavorful. If you must use this type of cucumber, slice and salt it for about 1 hour, and then rinse it prior to starting the pickling process. This will open the microscopic holes, letting the brine in.

Shriveled pickles may perhaps mean the white vinegar is too robust, the salt concentration too much, or the pickles over processed. Measure carefully watching the clock! Make sure to look at the recipe that you have in hand to ensure that all measurements are as accurate as possible. This will make all of the pickling processes that you do turn out so much better than if you disregard the directions.

Mixed flavors usually mean the length of the vegetables wasn't quite on. The larger the actual cut, the added time a vegetable takes acknowledge flavor. This is another time where you will have to take the time to look over your recipe to ensure that you have done it all correctly.

Mushy pickles can be a consequence of using the wrong kind of cucumber or over processing. You want to use cucumbers, preferably the lemon variety, small leaves, Edmonson, and Saladin. In order to increase the crispness of your vegetables, add grape leaves or use alum for food to the bottom of the jar.

Mold or dirt over a jar often implies it wasn't effectively sealed; some from the brine has got out onto the actual rim, meaning that bacteria can also get into the actual jar. Don't try to eat these. Whenever you're confronted by a jar people don't feel really right about, it's usually far better to err on the caution side of things and not eat it.

Chapter 5—Other Things to Preserves

So far you have just been given a short list of the different things that you are able to preserve using the various methods that are available and explained in this book. The things mentioned so far, such as fruits, vegetables, and meats, are not the only things that you are able to preserve in various forms. This chapter will provide you with some details on the various other things that you might be interested in learning how to preserve along with some recipes to get you started on it.

Condiments

Condiments are the first things that will be discussed in this chapter. There are many different types of condiments that you can make such as ketchup, mayonnaise, mustard, and even different types of relishes. The first part of this section is meant as an overview on how to properly store the condiments that you are making and then goes in to more about how to make them and finishes off with some recipes to try out.

To start us off with are the tomato based condiments that you might use. A popped open ketchup bottle can certainly last for ten or more months if stored inside your refrigerator, and 4 weeks if stored outside of the refrigerator. Vinegar can for at least a year if you do not open it and less time if you have opened it. Jarred salsas can keep in the refrigerator for about two months. Chili sauce can last for up to eight months, although Tabasco sauce can last for up to five years. Taco sauce can last for several years. Jarred jalapenos will last for about six months inside refrigerator.

Next off are the condiments that are often considered dairy condiments. Mayonnaise can last for up to six months in the freezer, while butter will only last for about fourteen days. Cream cheese will also last for about fourteen days. Margarine will last for about six months. Equally whipped cream and also sour cream have short shelf lives, at two days and three days, respectively. The condiment while using the shortest shelf life is hollandaise marinade. It will only last for a maximum of one day after opening it before the item expires and you will have to throw it away.

The next items are salad dressings. Most salad dressings will only last for a few days in the freezer. Ranch and bleu parmesan cheese dressings last approximately two months inside refrigerator. Thousand Island, French, and vinaigrette dressings also last for just two months in your refrigerator.

The rack lives of salsas vary greatly. Béarnaise can last for two days, while homemade garlic sauce will only last for 1 day. Cocktail sauce can last for six to eight months, while tartar marinade will expire after ninety days. Steak sauce lasts for up to a whole year if stored properly. Mustard stays edible for six to eight months. Worcestershire and soy marinade will both stay best for a year. Jams, jellies, preserves and maple syrup all last for any year in your refrigerator.

There are a wide variety of different condiments that you are able to use on the various foods that you consume. It is up to you to determine which ones you would like to include in your storage cabinet for the year to come. For some of the condiments, you will have to watch how much of them that you make and how many you open at once. They will not last all that long, even when properly preserved and stored and you do not want to waste out all of your hard work.

Creamy Pesto

2 chilies, jalapeno
2 cilantro bunches
2/3 c. pumpkin seeds, unsalted
¼ c. lime juice
4 garlic cloves
½ c. cheese, Mincho
1 c. oil, olive
Salt
Pepper

Take the seeds and the stems off the jalapenos along with any large stems that are on the cilantro. In the food processor you can take 2 of the garlic cloves and 1/3 cup pumpkin seeds and process them until they are finely chopped. Add in 2 Tbsp. lime juice, ½ cilantro, and 1 jalapeno. Process all of these together until they become a course puree. While the processor is still running, you can pour in about ½ c. of the oil and keep on processing. Spoon this pesto into a bowl and then repeat all of the steps with the rest of the ingredients. Stir the pepper, salt, and cheese in last. Store covered in the refrigerator.

Beef Gravy

1 lb. ground beef
3 Tbsp. flour, all purpose
½ c. onion
1 Tbsp. bouillon
2 c. milk
2 Tbsp. steak sauce

Take out a large skillet and cook together the onion and the ground beef until it has been cooked thoroughly, making sure to stir it around frequently. After the beef is done you can stir in the steak sauce, bouillon, and flour. Slowly add in the milk. Let it all cook together for about 6 minutes so that the mixture begins to thicken and boil. Make sure to continuously stir the mixture. Sever it over some rice or mashed potatoes if you wish once it has been completely cooked.

Jams and Preserves

The next type of thing that you might want to learn about preserving is jams and other preserves. In fact this is one of the most popular things that people will learn how to preserve. It is often easy to find a recipe that works for your needs and learning how to do it on your own opens up many more options for flavors and tastes. Often you will be stuck with maybe a handful of flavors if you go to the supermarket. If you learn how to make them on your own, you will be able to mix and match them any way that you want and your own limitation with are your own imagination.

Whether you are talking jam, preserves, jelly, conserves, or marmalades, they are all quite similar. This is because they are comprised of fruit with sugar, and are cooked until thick. Their individual characteristics depend on the kind of fruit used and the way it is prepared, the proportions of different ingredients in the mixture and the method of cooking.

Jellies are usually made by cooking fruit juice with sugar, although it is possible to make jelly without cooking, but that's a whole other story. A good product is clear and firm enough to hold its shape when turned out of the container, but quivers when the container is moved. When cut, it should be tender yet retain the angle of the cut. Jelly should have a flavorful, fresh, fruity taste.

Jams are thick; sweet spreads made by cooking crushed or chopped fruits with sugar. Jams tend to hold their shape but are generally less firm than jelly. The difference between jellies and jams is that the jellies you make or purchase will use fruit juices while the jams will use actual fruit.

Preserves are small, whole fruit or uniform size pieces in a clear, slightly gelled syrup. The fruit should be tender and plump. This means that they will use the whole fruit rather than the juice that comes from the fruit or mashing up the fruit that is in it. You will be able to get big chunks of fruit through this method.

Conserves are jam-like products that may be made with a combination of fruits. They also contain nuts, raisins or coconut. If you are interested in mixing and matching together different types of fruits in your preserving process, this is the type you will most likely be making.

Marmalades are soft fruit jellies containing small pieces of fruit or peel evenly suspended in the transparent jelly. They often contain citrus fruit.

Fruit butter, such as apple butter, honey, and syrup are all preserved with sugar, but do not contain gelatin. Fruit butters are made by reducing down the pulp of the fruit with sugar, until it is thick, yet spreadable. Honeys and syrups are made by cooking fruit juice or pulp with sugar to the consistency of honey or syrup.

Sweet spreads are a class of foods with many textures, flavors, and colors. They all consist of fruits preserved mostly by means of sugar and they are thickened or jellied to some extent. Fruit jelly is a semi-solid mixture of fruit juice and sugar that is clear and firm enough to hold its shape. Other spreads are made from crushed or ground fruit.

Jam also will hold its shape, but it is less firm than jelly. Jam is made from crushed or chopped fruits and sugar. Jams are comprised of a variety of different fruits, that when combined make what is called conserves. Some fruits used for jams include coconut, citrus fruits, and raisins. In addition, nuts are often used in jams.

Different from jams are preserves. This type of jelly includes pieces of fruit, or even whole fruit. The fruit is then placed in a thick, clear, jellied syrup. Although Marmalades have pieces of fruit, they are made in a transparent jelly. Even more different is fruit butter, which is made only from the pulp of the fruit and cooked down with sugar until the mixture is spreadable.

Intended for proper texture, jellied fruit products require the correct combination of berry, pectin, acid, in addition to sugar. The berry gives each distribute its unique flavor and color. It also supplies the lake to dissolve all of those other necessary ingredients in addition to furnishes some or the many pectin and acid. Good-quality, flavorful fruits make the best jellied products.

As was mentioned before, pectin is a very important ingredient to use in the process of preserving jams and preserves. Pectin's are elements in fruits in which form a gel when they are in the suitable combination with acid and sugar. Just about all fruits contain a number of pectin. Apples, crab oranges, gooseberries, and some plums and grapes typically contain enough natural pectin to make a gel. Some other fruits, such as strawberries, cherries, in addition to blueberries, contain little pectin and need to be combined with other fruits an excellent source of pectin or having commercial pectin products for getting gels. Because totally ripened fruit possesses less pectin, one-fourth with the fruit used for making jellies without added pectin need to be under ripe.

One thing to keep in mind is that commercially frozen in addition to canned juices could be low in normal pectin's and make soft textured spreads.

The proper degree of acidity is critical to gel development. If there is low acid, the gel will not set; if there is too much acid, the gel will miss liquid (weep). For fruits lower acid, add orange juice or additional acid ingredients as directed. Commercial pectin products contain acids that assist to ensure gelling.

Sugar serves as being a preserving agent, contributes flavor, and supports gelling. Cane and beet sugar will be the usual sources involving sugar for jelly or jam. Corn syrup and honey enable you to replace part with the sugar in quality recipes, but too considerably will mask the actual fruit flavor in addition to alter the teeth whitening gel structure. Use tried recipes for updating sugar with honey and corn syrup. Do not seek to reduce the volume of sugar in regular recipes. Too little sugar prevents gelling and will allow yeasts and molds growing.

It is also possible to make jams and preserves without sugar if that is what your dietary guidelines state for your health. Jellies and jams that include modified pectin, gelatin, or gums could be made with no caloric sweeteners. Jams with a smaller amount sugar than usual also could be made with focused fruit pulp, which in turn contains less fluid and less sugar.

Two types involving modified pectin are available for home use. Just one gels with one-third a smaller amount sugar. The other is a low-methoxyl pectin which requires a source of calcium for gelling. To stop spoilage, jars of the products must always be processed longer inside a boiling-water canner. Recipes and processing times supplied with each modified pectin product need to be followed carefully. The proportions involving acids and fruits should not be altered, as spoilage might result.

Acceptably gelled fridge fruit spreads also could be made with gelatin in addition to sugar substitutes. Like products spoil on room temperature, need to be refrigerated, and need to be eaten within 1 month.

Although sugar helps preserve jellies and jellies, molds can grow at very fast paces on these products. Research now indicates that the mold which persons usually scrape from the surface of jellies may not be as harmless the way it seems. Mycotoxins are actually found in a number of jars of jelly having surface shape growth. Mycotoxins are recognized as causes of cancer inside animals; their effects on humans remain being researched.

Because of possible mold toxins, paraffin or soy wax seals are no longer recommended for almost any sweet spread, such as jellies. To prevent expansion of molds and decrease in good flavor or color, fill products hot into clean Mason jars, departing 1/4-inch headspace, close off with self-sealing lids, and process 5 minutes inside a boiling-water canner. Correct process period at higher elevations with the help of 1 additional minute per 1, 000 legs above sea amount. If unsterile jars are used, the filled jars need to be processed 10 units. Use of clean jars is recommended, especially when fruits are lower pectin, since the added in 5-minute process time could potentially cause weak gels.

There are two basic methods that you can use for making jams, jellies and preserves in your own home. The normal method, which will not require added pectin, is most effective with fruits naturally an excellent source of pectin. The additional method, which requires the use of commercial liquid or powdered pectin, is much quicker. The gelling ability of numerous pectin's differs. To generate uniformly gelled products, be sure to provide the quantities involving commercial pectin's to help specific fruits as instructed on just about every package. Overcooking may digest pectin and reduce proper gelling. When you use either method, make one batch each time, according to the actual recipe. Increasing the quantities often ends in soft gels. Stir constantly while cooking to counteract burning. Recipes tend to be developed for certain jar sizes. If jellies are packed into larger jars, exceedingly soft products might result.

Tutti Frutti Jam

3 c. pears, chopped
¾ c. pineapple, crushed
1 orange
¼ c. cherries, maraschino
¼ c. lemon juice
5 c. sugar
1 pkg. pectin, powdered

You can start out my measuring the pears so that they fit into the kettle. Add in the lemon juice, cherries, pineapple, and orange next before stirring in the pectin. Place it all on a high heat setting. While it is cooking, you will want to stir it until it becomes a full boil. At this time you can add in the sugar and continue on with the stirring. Let it continue boiling for about 1 minute before taking off the heat and skimming the top. Fill up the jars with the jam right away, making sure to leave some room at the top. Wipe the jars with some paper towels before placing the lids on top. Process the cans with some boiling water either in a kettle or a pressure cooker.

Strawberry Preserves
4 ½ c. of sugar

6 c. strawberries, prepared

Make sure that when you are picking out the berries to use with this preserve that you pick ones that are nice and fresh. If you use ones that are not the greatest you will end up with the whole batch being bad. Combine together the sugar and the fruit using alternate layers. Let them both set for about 10 hours in a cool place. The next day you can pour out the mixture into a saucepan and bring it all to a boil, making sure to stir it the whole time. Let it start boiling rapidly while stirring to prevent any sticking from occurring. You will want to continue letting it boil until it has become thick. At this time you can take it off the heat and skim off the extras on the top. Fill up the jars with the hot preserves right away. Make sure to leave a little bit of room on the top of the jar. Wipe off the rims with a paper towel before placing the two pieces lids on top. Process the cans before storing.

Marinades

The next thing that you might be interested in learning how to preserve is marinades. These are always great to use on meats and even vegetables. Whether you are grilling out in your backyard or just want to add in a little bit more flavor to your meats, marinades are certainly the way to go.

The primary marinades, before refrigeration, were employed to preserve the quality meats that were eaten. It was used as another form of preservation in place of using the drying method. While the drying method was good for taking foods on a long journey, perhaps traveling across the whole country, marinades might be better suited for home use if you would like the meat to last a little bit longer. The marinade that you would put on the meat would often help to enhance the flavor. And with all of the flavors that are available to use for a marinade, you would be able to mix and match to find your favorite and change it up with every meal.

The following marinates work very well on most reduces of meats. The bigger the roast or amount of meat, the longer it needs marinating to penetrate and tenderize. This means that if you have a large roast that you are trying to marinate, you might find that it is going to take you a day or two in order to let the marinades seep in and flavor the meat. On the other hand, if you are simply marinating a few pieces of regular sized chicken, you might do just fine with throwing them in the sauce and letting them set for a few hours or even overnight.

Marinades are typically comprised of acids, oils, and herbs or spices. Natural oils are used for to protect and preserve the foods, as well as transfer the flavor from the marinade to what it is you are marinating. Acids, such as wines and lemon or vegetable juice help soften the foods texture and breakdown connective tissue generating the meat more tender even though the herbs or spices impart plenty of flavor. The length of time for an excellent marinate depends on the length of the item and also the desired taste. If you would like the meat to just have a hint of the taste on it, you will only need to let it set for a short while. If you would like the meat to have a full blast of the flavor and be overwhelmed by it you might have to let it set for a much longer time. You can look to your recipe for help on this matter or you can experiment a little to find the best method for your tastes.

One thing to keep in mind about the products that you use for the marinate process includes: It is advisable to use metal bowls and metal pans for marinating meals, also many tools can be found to help together with marinates (like the jacquard tenderizer).

You do not have to just make a sauce in order to have a marinade. Often, a dry rub will work just as well and you might find that it is much easier for storage and preservation. A dry marinate can be called a dry rub, it is an assortment of salt, pepper, herbs and spices and it's used on lean meats. Sometimes oil as well as other liquid is added to manufacture a paste to chafe onto the lean meat.

There are many things that you can use marinades for and they have started to become really popular with those that like a little extra something with their meats and even those who are big fans of grilling. Some people like the marinades because they are much healthier to eat than putting dressings or other things on top of their chicken or other meat products.

You do not have to be a master chef in order to make a marinade or learn how to preserve one of your very own. There are tons of recipes online that you can use so that you can find one that meets your tastes. Even if you have been to a restaurant that serves a sauce or marinade that you simply love, you might be able to find that exact recipe online, or at least one that is similar. Take the time to look around and see what is available. Mix and match and try some new things out so that you can find your new favorite blend.

The following are a few marinade recipes that you can try out to see if they will soon become one of your new favorites.

Savory Marinade

2 cloves of garlic
1 Tbsp. sugar
4 oz. wine, red
1 Tbsp. hot sauce
4 oz. water
1 rosemary sprig
2 oz. olive oil
1 lemon

Take the lemon and cut it in half and then juice it. Get rid of the rind and all of the stuff except the juice. Next take the cloves of garlic and cut them up as well. Get out a medium sized bowl and mix together the garlic, sugar, red wine, hot sauce, water, rosemary sprigs, olive oil, and lemon. Place the meat into the bowl to marinate. This mixture is good for marinating a 2 pound roast. You will need to vary the ingredients to fit based on the amount of food that you are using the marinate on. If you are using the 2 pound roast, you will need to let it set in the refrigerator overnight so that it has time to absorb up all of the flavors. Vary the time it sets in the marinade depending on how strong you want the flavor. Take it out the next day and grill or roast it up to enjoy.

Garlic Marinade

1 Tbsp. soy sauce
2 cloves of garlic
4 oz. water
1 Tbsp. brown sugar
3 oz. sherry

Bring out a bowl and toss together the soy sauce, garlic cloves, water, brown sugar, and the sherry. You can always tweak the flavors a little bit to get them exactly how you want them. This recipe is meant for a 2 pound roast so you may have to alter it a bit to get the right amount for the amount of meat that you are cooking up. Once the marinade is done, you can add in the meat to the bowl and then cover it up and place it in the refrigerator. The amount of time that you leave it in will depend on how much meat you are trying to marinade and how strong you would like the flavor to turn out. Make sure that while the meat is in the refrigerator you turn it around a few times to get the flavor everywhere.

There are many different types of preserving methods that are available for you to try out. Many of them have been around since the beginning of time as a method of keeping meats and other foods good for the long journeys across land and sea. It just was not possible to take all of that food along with them wherever they were going and so they had to come up with methods that would work for the easy transportation of these food products.

The main types of food preservation that are available include canning, freezing, drying, and pickling. Each has been discussed in some detail throughout this book in the hopes that you will understand when to use each one and would gain a basic understanding of how each process works. Some of them will work out much better with certain products while others you might want to stay away from. You might also be able to determine which one works the best for you depending on the taste that you would like to get out of the whole process.

Learning how to preserve can be an event that you can enjoy no matter who you are. Many people who choose to try out some of these methods will have their own farms or at least gardens, although this is certainly not a requirement for starting the preserving process. While growing your own food products will help to ensure that they are nice and fresh and of the best quality that is available, purchasing the store food products is certainly fine if that is the only option that is available to you. Some people are too busy to tend to a whole garden all of the time and they might live in a city without any room to give it all the proper attention. You can always make modifications to make it work with your busy lifestyle.

If you are looking to get into the preserving world, take the time to read through this guidebook to learn more about the different methods that will work and see how well they will work out for you. Read the directions carefully to help ensure that you are doing everything correctly and that all of your food will stay preserved how it is supposed to. It can be disappointing to spend all of that hard work on this project just to find out that you did it completely wrong and have to waste out all of the products.

Preserving food can be a fun activity to do and can give you a sense of pride once you have gotten down the whole process and understand what you are supposed to do. Take the time to learn a few new things today and be surprised at all the amazing things that you can do.

www.ingramcontent.com/pod-product-compliance
Lightning Source LLC
LaVergne TN
LVHW070943211224
799667LV00013B/1254